KINGDOM BUSINESS: LICENSED TO LEAD

KINGDOM BUSINESS: LICENSED TO LEAD

KEVIN J. SUBER

© 2019 by Kevin Suber
All rights reserved. This book or any portion thereof may not be reproduced or used in any manner whatsoever without the express written permission of the publisher except for the use of brief quotations in a book review.

ISBN: 9781792154607

*This book is dedicated to my amazing wife, who ensured it would be completed;
to my children, who are my pride and joy and my gift to the future;
to Luis Lopez, who showed up every week with recorder in hand to make
sure the words were captured.*

Thank you.

TABLE OF CONTENTS

Introduction	ix
Definitions of a Kingdom	1
Gifts and Talents	7
Your Why: Why Lead? Why Build?	11
The Vision	15
Execution	19
Leadership	23
Overcoming Challenges	28
Suber's Story	35
The Four Pillars: Your Foundation	37
Legacy	42
Glossary of Suggested Reading	45
Acknowledgments	47
Author Bio	49

INTRODUCTION

Kingdom business: Who am I? Well, obviously I'm Kevin Suber. Why would I write a book? Well, why not write a book? Every time I speak to people, they say, "Wait a minute—hold up. You did that?" What person goes to engineering school and ten years later just stops? What person grows up in Connecticut and willingly goes to the South? Who does that? When I think about the whole process and the footsteps in the pathway of where my life has been, I realize several things; number one is that this entire time, I have been perfectly prepared for my purpose.

Every single thing that happened to me did one of two things: it either redirected me or grew and educated me. So I'm thankful for every single thing that has happened because that is the reason why I can actually speak to you and introduce myself to you right now.

I'm the guy who grew up in New England but who loves all things international. I'm the guy who grew up with his mother and father, while many of his friends didn't grow up with theirs. I'm that guy.

I'm the guy who understands and loves and embraces so much from so many people, from so many different cultures. I'm a guy who has done a whole lot compared to some others with respect to doing business in and outside of the United States. I'm that guy. By faith, I know what happened, but logically, I don't even know how it happened—it just happened.

I'm a guy who fell into speaking but absolutely loves every single word that comes out because I know it's not from me; it's not necessarily for me, but it's for other people. I'm that guy.

I'm a guy who has done discipleship groups and done a wedding and done a funeral, but I'm also the guy who's done business in Thailand and done business in Canada and done business in Bermuda and done business in the UK. I'm that guy.

So why would *you* listen to *that* guy? Why not listen to that guy?

Because all of us could probably see a little bit of ourselves in that guy and get something from that guy. So that's who Kevin Suber is. And I think as you continue to examine that, you'll quickly understand why I wrote this book.

Kingdom business. Everybody has a vision. Everybody has something that's inside of him or her, but people don't always know how to get those things out of themselves. And my kingdom and your kingdom could be two very different kingdoms, yet a kingdom must be built. Your kingdom must be built! You must lead with integrity and passion under all circumstances!

For some people, the kingdom is really just the kingdom of God. For some people, the kingdom is this business idea that they always wanted to do, and they don't even know where to start. For some people, the kingdom is this: I've got this way that I know could bring world peace. I've got this thing in me that I know can help so many children, but I don't even know where to start. Your kingdom is not my kingdom, yet kingdoms must be built.

The one thing that we all must understand is that because one kingdom exists, it does not mean that another kingdom cannot exist, but these two kingdoms—or three or four, or ten, or one thousand kingdoms—can coexist and work together, yet individual kingdoms can be built. They, in fact, must be built.

Kingdom Business: Licensed to Lead is the title of the book. The kingdom. People have many different thoughts when you say "the kingdom." Before we can have a real discussion on kingdom business, we have to first define what the kingdom is because the kingdom can mean different things for different people.

A kingdom could be a politically organized community or major territorial unit that has a monarchical form of government headed by a king or queen. That's *Merriam-Webster's* definition. The kingdom is the love of God prevailing in politics, in business, in government, and in media. It is the impact of the laws of God creating a social environment, where the strong help the weak and where those who have give to those who don't.

It's a society where relationships are built on love; that's what Myles Munroe said. You make kingdoms and castles on your own—that's what Stephan Jenkins said. All of the great empires of the future will be empires of the mind—that's what Winston Churchill said.

There are many different perspectives on the kingdom, but all of them basically lead to a process of building something that is bigger than ourselves. When you think of a kingdom, you think "regal." When you think of a kingdom, you think "everlasting." When you think of a kingdom, you think "legacy." All great kings are remembered not just for what they built but also for what they left behind. So, when I think of kingdom business, I believe it certainly can be a business—the legacy of that business that you leave behind—but it doesn't have to be business related.

There is a process that you're going to learn as you walk through this book. The things that you're going to be exposed to are based on my pathway—the lessons learned in my pathway through life that you can extract and use to get what you need out of the call on your life. If that happens when you get through this book, then that's a beautiful thing. That's the goal. That is why anybody would read this book.

So that's why you should read this book; that is exactly what I want you to get out of this.

As we go through this book, you'll see more in-depth information on developing your leadership so that your kingdom will be revealed. You're going to see more in-depth information on your gifts and your talents. You'll see more in-depth information on the call—that is, the call on your life. So many times, we feel this passion, something burning inside of us that we know that we must accomplish. That's the call on your life. But the call is incomplete without recognizing why you should do something and without then attaching vision to that. Then, once you have the vision, you've got to execute that vision. Got it?

These are some of the things that you'll walk through in this book. You're also going to walk through not just the concept of what a kingdom is, but you're going to walk through what comprises your own kingdom.

Your kingdom and my kingdom, as I mentioned earlier, could be two separate things. You are going to learn how to overcome challenges, and then you're going to learn how to be that leader that you are called to be. And remember, you can overcome challenges without being a leader, but you certainly cannot be a leader without having the ability to overcome challenges.

When we get to the end of this book, we're going to have a conversation about legacy. And when that's done, you will have snatched the pebble from my hand, and it will be time for you to leave—time for you to go lead and build your own kingdom.

So welcome to the ride. Put your seat belt on. Here we go.

DEFINITIONS OF A KINGDOM

Kingdom business. We've been talking about kingdom business. Before we can dig into the concept of a kingdom, we must fully understand the different perspectives, the different definitions. I want to dig into that just a bit. Whatever your perspective, whatever you think about what a kingdom is by definition or what a kingdom can mean to you, I wanted to give some perspective so that you can have a foundation to build on when you're considering kingdom business or building your kingdom.

Merriam-Webster's defines a kingdom as "a politically organized community or a major territorial unit having a monarchial form of government headed by a king or queen."

We've seen historically that some kings and some queens have significant amounts of wisdom, and they're remembered through the ages for that wisdom. There were some kings and queens who came into power with not so much wisdom and not so much foresight and without the skill sets for leadership or managing people. And those kingdoms fell and will continue to fall.

That is certainly one definition of what a kingdom is and what a kingdom could mean for you as we discover kingdom business.

Myles Munroe has another perspective: the kingdom is the love of God prevailing in politics and business and government and media. It is the impact of the laws of God creating a social environment where the strong help the weak, where those who have given to those who don't. It's a society where relationships are built on love.

Basically, Myles Munroe is taking a portion of what *Merriam-Webster's* has defined for a kingdom with respect to government, but he expands on that definition as he takes it into politics and business—he takes it into government and media (we'll talk later in this book about your gifts and talents). Myles Munroe basically said that this is your kingdom; your kingdom may be so expansive that it spreads beyond the normal mind-set of what a kingdom is.

I like that definition, because for me, whatever kingdom you're building should affect not just you but also other people. Like Munroe's expansive definition, your leadership should have the ability to be lasting. As you're serving your kingdom, your kingdom should also be serving you with respect to growing you. The perfect kingdom has a reciprocal flow where you serve and you are served. Make no mistake—as a leader, your focus should be serving, and the byproducts of your laser focus on serving are your growth and expansion. This growth and expansion will feel like you are being served. This is why I like Munroe's perspective; he's talking about something that expands beyond you, something that serves people but does not intentionally serve self. Serve oneself only with respect to self-care and to growing yourself so that you can then serve at a higher level. This I love. I also love the definition that Stephan Jenkins gives because it's simple and yet very, very important.

Ultimately when you finish reading this book, I want you to feel like you can start, grow, and build a kingdom that will continue to build upon itself and ultimately leave a legacy. Stephan Jenkins keeps it really simple: he says you make kingdoms and castles on your own. What this meant to me is that you must decide to start. You must decide to lead. You must decide to build!

Jim Rohn is somebody whom I love and read and listen to; I watch many of his videos. One of the topics he consistently talks about is *philosophy*. Any person can change where he or she is in life in five years based on two things: whom the person associates with and what the person reads. Those who surround you and what you read are 100 percent dependent on and impacted by your philosophy. So when you evaluate kingdom building or moving or growing from one space to another, ultimately it's a castle, and it's a kingdom that you built on your own.

You will make a decision, or you have made a decision. You will get mad or you got mad. Like you got MAD—you Made A Decision, you wanted to Make A Difference. MAD—eternally MAD!

This is what you chose to do, and once you made that decision, you can then, on your own, build and grow a kingdom, but it's something that you have to make a conscious decision to do. Once you make that conscious decision to build and grow something—that's where the magic happens.

That's where the kingdom starts getting built, that's where the kingdom starts growing, and that's where kingdom expands, ultimately until it becomes something that serves many, many people. I have seen this in the United States and around the world over and over again! *You* will do this! Kingdom business.

We're talking about kingdom business. I love what Winston Churchill said; it is almost as simple as what Stephan Jenkins said, yet it moves the definition of *kingdom* to a different space. It moves it away from the physicality of the action items and the steps that you have to take. He says, "All the great empires of the future will be empires of the mind."

I love this because ultimately, we all—as we think about a kingdom, as we think about what we do on a day-to-day basis—must understand that our thoughts become real if we don't limit ourselves. Our thoughts will *also* become real if we do limit ourselves. Let me repeat this because this is important: our thoughts become real if we choose not to limit ourselves. We are only limited by our fear; we are only limited by the things that we have grown to believe based on societal constructs or pressures.

There are things that families and friends have done over time that made us doubt what we knew was fact in our hearts, what we knew hit our spirit strongly. We knew it was the truth, but then life happened, and then we started to doubt. Stop doubting—you were right!

You were born with a gift. You were born with a song, and the song must be sung. If you don't sing your song—if your song is not sung—then no one gets impacted by that song. All some folks need to recognize their calling is a sing-along! *Sing your song!* I'm singing mine now…and…I can hear some of you singing with me as you read the words that you're reading right now.

The kingdom. All the great empires of the future will be empires of the mind. If you can think it, if you can dream it, then you can do it. The resources exist simply because it crossed your mind. Don't ever doubt the power of the gift of what can be implanted as a seed that can grow from your thoughts. First, you're humming…then you sing along, and then you are on stage singing your song! Your gifts are powerful—they are divine in nature—and they will make room for you!

Ultimately, to build your kingdom, two things are critical. Number one, you must have a strong foundation. Number two, to build your kingdom you must have leadership. Leadership skills must be possessed by you!

We're going to talk about that foundation. I have named my perspective on that foundation "the four pillars." The four pillars are the cornerstones of leadership. One of those four pillars is how you deal with health and wellness. One of them is how you deal with your spiritual life. One of those four pillars is how you deal with your vocation, your business, your job. The last of those four pillars is how you deal with interpersonal skills—dealing with the people who are around you. We are all the results of how we handle the four pillars, and they set the foundations of our own personal kingdoms, no matter what decisions we made. No matter what we decide to do to make a difference, the four pillars create the vehicle we will drive, so let's create the best vehicle and drive it.

Yes, we all have gifts and talents, but at the end of the day, without properly managing and growing the four pillars (which ultimately make the foundation), we will have challenges. Faith and mind-set are the starting points, if you will, of building your kingdom. Without faith and mind-set, it's impossible for your kingdom to be that expansive—that living, that ever-growing kingdom that leaves a legacy, that impacts so many beyond you. Winston Churchill said, "The great empires will be empires of the mind." So have a kingdom mind-set knowing this. As you are reading this (and hopefully and prayerfully getting inspired), the empire of your mind will give you peace, spark your passion, and build your foundation and leadership.

Leadership is so critical in building a kingdom as well. With these cornerstones, your kingdom will have growth, impact, and expansion. Without leadership, your kingdom cannot be built. At best you are simply assembling people and resources. Leadership and a foundation—that is how you will build your kingdom.

Notes

Which definition of *kingdom* is closest to how you define *kingdom*?

How do you define *kingdom*?

Are you MAD? What made you MAD?

Are you afraid of the burden of building your kingdom?

If you had unlimited resources, what kingdom would you build?

GIFTS AND TALENTS

Gifts and talents are probably the most important things that start this process of building your kingdom.

We must begin understanding what our gifts are. We must begin using the talents we have developed (and they are different than gifts). Our gifts are truly things that are given to us. Talent is something that maybe you have a proclivity for, or an interest in, that can be significantly developed. A gift is just what you inherently possess. Some people are gifted speakers. They do it so well they can do it at the drop of a dime. You tell them, "Give me five minutes," and they can go.

That's a gift. A teacher's a gift. Again, some people simply have ways of communicating.

A way of reaching. A way of impacting. A way of showing people the power that they possess. That gift of teaching is an incredible gift. But a talent for administration is something that can be developed as a talent over time. You can take many, many classes, and actually those teachers with gifts can then show you how to utilize your talents. Recognizing both your gifts and talents and using them is very, very important.

That tug, that pull, that you feel daily, that drives you like an engine and guides you like a compass—it's not an accident. It's by design. It's by divine design. It is a gift from above. Let's be clear: there's a call in your life.

There's both power and authority that accompanies this call. Congratulations.

You've also been equipped for this journey. Make no mistake: you are gifted. You're gifted. If you can accept this, everything changes.

You're different, unique, because your call is different. Your call is unique. Accept and embrace the nuances of your divine design, and go forth with the power, conviction, and authority that has been gathering in the recesses of your life. It's time to dust it off.

Remember this: you are destined for impact. Today, cast out all fear and anxiety, for neither fear nor anxiety can produce love. In fact, perfect love drives out fear; therefore, all we do must be done in love. Cast out every negative or uncertain thought that you had up to the moment you started reading this. You are called. Embrace the call.

Use your gifts. Make an impact. Start today.

During my study, I read something interesting from one of the apostles, the Apostle Paul. He said he had received a special gift in proportion to what Christ has given. (For those Bible scholars who are reading this, if you want to look it up, it can be found in Ephesians 4:7).

What struck me is how he talked about the gift, the special gift, so we know that it is special. You, your uniqueness, your gift—they are special and different. Your gift is for you to use. But what's interesting is that he said it's in proportion to what Christ has given. This hit me because it means that everybody is going to have impact. The question is, what are we impacting?

If your impact is on your block or in your house, don't ever feel that it's less than the impact of the person that becomes a councilperson, a governor, a president, or a pope. For the world to be a better place, for our kingdoms to be perfectly built in all its imperfections, we all—each and every single one of us—must embrace our gifts and our talents and realize that the portions that we are given are the portions that we need to have. Those portions are given so that we can impact exactly what or exactly whom we are supposed to impact.

It could be that there is simply one person that you have to reach. It might only be one person, but this one person is designed to reach hundreds of thousands of people in a very different way. But if you don't do your part, that person can never, ever, ever do his or her part. So we all must embrace the portions of the gifts and the portions of the talents that we have—not just so that we can grow, so that we can walk in peace and power, but so that the ones who were designated also answer the calls regarding the purposes of their lives. It is important that we simply do our parts. When we do our parts and others do theirs, that's the gift, and that's the importance of using both our gifts and our talents.

Notes

Have you been called gifted or talented?

What is/are your gift(s)?

What is/are your talent(s)?

What is stopping you from activating your gifts and talents?

YOUR WHY: WHY LEAD? WHY BUILD?

I'm a father, and I have four children: two boys and two girls. Any parent has heard one single question more than any other question. And that question is, "Why?" Why is up, up? Why is down, down? Why are you my father? Why is there a God? Why is there not a God? Why can't I see him? Why do I not feel him? Why do we live here? Why are we going there? "Why" is the question that is always, always asked. We use our knowledge of "why" in the framework of kingdom building and kingdom business. Your why is the way you're going to put that together.

Your why will be your compass. I don't mean the question "Why?" from a child's perspective (although the freshness with which a child asks that question is probably important with respect to maintaining your passion). Children never get tired of asking the question, and if you're building your kingdom, your "why" is something that should always remain fresh to you. It's a question that you should always ask and always evaluate on a daily basis. Your why is what drives you. Get in the habit of reminding yourself *why* you're doing what you're doing.

Your why is the engine to your soul, and it is the compass to your mind. Your why gives you the energy to go. Your why gives you the direction in which to go.

As we continue with this message, we truly understand and know how to put everything together—the sum of all of the aforementioned components is your why. Earlier, we spoke about your gifts and talents and now, your why. Both gifts and talents and your why are very different things for many people. But ultimately your why is what makes you get out of bed every single day.

The reality is some days that we just feel like lying there, if we're being honest. Now we certainly don't have to be honest, but let's try honesty. The why is our daily alarm clock. The why is our battle cry. The why is the canvas on which the murals of our lives are illustrated! I had a mentor in business who told me if your why doesn't make you cry, it's not big enough. I had a conversation with a client who realized he had no idea why he wanted to start a new venture. He understood that it was something that he should be doing. He even understood the impact on his household with respect to his time, freedom, and wealth, as well as ultimately leaving a legacy for his household.

Based on his conversations, and looking at his track record, I figured out what his struggle was; he had a history of starting projects and not finishing them. His struggle was finding out the breakthrough that makes him go beyond anything he had ever done before. How could he finish what he started?

As we continued to talk, he realized that there was one thing he wanted to do more than anything else in his life, but not until we had that dialogue did he realize what drove him as well as what would help him finish. He realized the one thing he had never thought about before, and it was at that moment he realized that one thing was the engine to his soul. That one thing was the compass to his mind, and that was the one thing that was going to have him continue to go forward when he had those days where people weren't necessarily understanding or friendly to his purpose. Pop culture was his passion! Now all that he does revolves around pop culture, and his why has been resurrected.

At the end of the day, your purpose is your purpose. People don't have to cooperate with your purpose. We have to drive our purposes. We all have purposes. We all have gifts; we all have talents. Regarding your why, what is that thing that would make you continue working on building your kingdom when the resources are not there? What is the thing that would get you to continue building your kingdom when you hit the wall? What is the thing that makes you work when you're tired? What is the thing that makes you study when you don't feel like studying? What is the thing that makes you get out of bed? What is that thing? That is your why.

For some people, a why might be, "I'm going to increase my income streams and give my spouse the option to retire." For some people, a why is, "I want to travel—I want to see Bangladesh, I want to see Bali, I want to see Botswana." That's their thing. Their thing is that they view themselves as world citizens, and so that drives them; the why that drives them is the ability to have this freedom to travel at the drop of a dime.

What is your why? What makes you get up in the morning? What makes you focus? What makes you push? What makes you press on every single day when you're tired?

Clearly defining your why and clearly understanding the impact of what that means—not just for you, but for other people—is what should happen when you finish reading this chapter. When you clearly define your why and you understand that your why must be big enough to make you cry, it's at that moment you take the key and open the door; you're ready to progress to the next stage.

Notes

What is your why? Who makes you want to be better?

What is a cause that you would give anything for? Why?

Who would you do anything for? Why?

Does the thought of not accomplishing your why make you anxious, or does it give you focus?

THE VISION

As I write this part of the book and go through what I want to say about vision, it is the beginning of the year. This is a very interesting time of the year to watch people.

I'm a walker. Occasionally I run. Whether I am walking or running, I get up early in the morning mainly because it's my routine; there's a routine that I like to keep on a daily basis that keeps me on point. Consistency at the beginning of my day sets the tone for the rest of it. I always notice this time of year there's always more people out there because everyone has great vision at the beginning of the year about what his or her year is going to look like. Sometimes that vision comes from talking to somebody or seeing other people, but it usually comes in the form of a New Year's resolution. Whatever gets you to the point of that vision, the most important thing you can do is actually have vision.

When you hear me speak, when you hear me in conversation with people, when you see some things I've written, you'll notice that I talk about being thankful. No matter where you are right now, you could always be somewhere else that is less desirable than where you are. I have always believed a thankful heart is critical to your sense of peace; a thankful, grateful heart not only is critical to peace of mind but is also critical to your vision.

It's hard to see a future if you can't see how far you've come and if you don't even understand where you are. And gratitude is a big deal for me. I love what Melody Beattie said: "Gratitude makes sense of our past, brings peace for today, and creates a vision for tomorrow." It's important to understand that you must be thankful for every single thing you have in order to even wrap your arms around—wrap your head around, wrap your mind around—having vision.

Let me say it another way: vision is impossible without being thankful. You cannot see the future if you don't understand what got you to where you are and why you are where you are. Be thankful for the present, where we are right now. There are two ways to look at it: "My life has been so difficult (or these moments have been so difficult); my gosh, I can't take it" or "I have learned so much that it's gotten me to this point where I am right now." These are two very different perspectives.

Of course, there are nuances and all that, but those two perspectives will define and determine how you move forward, how you start to build your kingdom. I would implore you to be thankful for every single thing that has gotten you to where you are right now. Being thankful will have you at peace, which will help to create a vision, and our visions are frequently driven by our dreams.

Keep your dreams alive. Understand that achieving anything requires faith and belief in yourself, vision, hard work, determination, and dedication. Remember that Gail Devers says, "All things are possible for those who believe."

Let's keep on vision. Let's keep on faith. In order to carry a positive action, we must develop here a positive vision. Those words are from the Dalai Lama. Vision again—I must drive this point home. Vision is impossible without peace about where we are right now. If you see and hear me speak, you know that I love the philosophy of Jim Rohn. I love the way that Brian Tracy speaks about progress and philosophy.

I had a conversation with a young man I mentor this morning, and he thanked me for a book that I had given him. He said it's already changed his life, and I said, "Great. Bring it back; I'll give you another one." He continued, "No, you don't understand. My vision is completely different now." I guess that's why I saw him—because my conversation today is about vision. I could tell there was a peace about him and even more of a sense of purpose, and that's what drives us toward the future.

Having peace where you are right now and purpose driving your vision, you must always keep your dreams alive. When your dreams are kept alive, that is when you can fully embrace vision. That is when our eyes are wide open and we can truly see into the future—not just where we are, where we're going to go, where we need to go, and how we can impact the lives of others.

Vision. Future. Future. Vision.

Eleanor Roosevelt said, "The future belongs to those who believe in the beauty of their dreams." So let's recap our conversation. To be at peace, we must be thankful; we must be filled with gratitude for where we are. And if we're filled with gratitude from where we are, then we have peace. That peace allows us to dream, and for some it's actually to dream again. Once you're a dreamer filled with purpose (and you understand why, as we had the discussion about your why), those elements allow you to drive your thoughts into the future. Driving your thoughts into the future does two things: it creates your future, and it also creates vision.

My words for you today and right here: be thankful for every single thing that has happened to you in your life. Embrace the beauty of your dreams; they create your future and your vision.

Notes

What are you passionate about?

What task/deed/project do you think about frequently?

If your gifts and talents were perfected, what would you do?

If money were no object, what would you be doing right now?

EXECUTION

Execution. If you say the word *execution* by itself, it can actually have a negative, daunting connotation. The executioner. You're going to be executed. An execution has taken place.

The reality is that to build your kingdom, to do something great, once you've gone through the process of why are you doing this and defined what your vision is, you must then execute the vision.

Execution must take place. If it helps to think of something negative, think of killing the distractions, think of killing and executing all those things that would actually prevent you from getting started.

I sat with a client yesterday, and it was interesting because first off, he said, "Kev, I'm grateful for you." That's always a good thing. "I'm grateful for you because had I not sat down with you, I wouldn't even know where to begin executing this vision I have. I don't even know where to start. That is my biggest challenge: where to start. I got these mountains. I've got these big dreams. These things I want to happen, but I don't know where to start." And I understand that because I've been in a similar position.

Nikki Sixx is a bass player. You don't know who he is? Look him up. Nikki Sixx says, "I've got so many mountains to climb and goals to conquer. I've got so many scars I want to leave on the planet, but I feel like I'm not there yet. I feel like I'm just getting started."

When it comes to kingdom building, when it comes to doing something phenomenal, so many people they feel like they're not there yet. Maybe they feel like they're not prepared yet. Maybe they feel they're not worthy of this big vision that they've been given. Yet we all know the difference between those who do great things and those who do not do great things (whatever the definition of a *great thing* is for them or for those evaluating them). But they all did one thing that somebody else did not: they got started. That's it!

All they did was they got started. We sometimes go through this all year and say, "I don't know how to get started" because we're thinking too much. Mark Twain said the secret of getting ahead is getting started. It's as simple as that.

Want to get ahead? Get started.

You will make mistakes. That's okay. Start.

There might be more to do than you expected. That's okay. Start.

You might trip, stumble, fall. That is okay. Start.

You're uncomfortable. Okay. Start.

You're not ready. Okay. Start.

The difference between you impacting at least one person and you impacting only yourself is to start. That is it.

Start. Start now. *Start right now!*

We think there has to be all this information and all this planning. Information and planning are both good, but it doesn't matter if you don't start. You must start.

Execution lies in the ability to say, "Today, I start." Zig Ziglar stated, "You don't have to be great to get started, but you do have to start to be great."

If you have a dream, you can spend a lifetime studying, planning, and getting ready for it. What you should be doing is getting started. My friend, you must start. And when you start, you have to run to your destiny. Start and then run. Run like it's midnight and it's the last bus of the night and you have no money in your pocket. And all you have is a bus pass, and that bus is five blocks away, and you have thirty seconds to get there.

Get started, and run. Run to your destiny!

It is necessary for execution simply to get started. How do you execute? Number one, you start. Number two, continue. When you start, you can't stop. When you start, you must persevere.

When you start, you must keep going. So you must start and continue, and don't quit.

Perseverance is necessary; a mind-set is necessary. Start. Continue. (And continuation's cousin is named tenacity—don't quit.) Start and continue. If you put those together, you've defined perseverance.

Samuel Johnson said, "Great works are performed not by strength, but by perseverance." Persevere, my friends.

Thomas Jefferson said, "When we see ourselves in a situation which must be endured, it is best to make up our minds to it. Meet it with firmness and accommodate everything to it in the best way practical. This lessens the evil while threading and fuming only serves to increase your own torments." (I may be a little partial to him as I am a UVA grad.) But he's speaking about persevering.

You must go and commit to finishing this. Don't quit. Continue and don't quit. Finally, execution lies in knowing when you start that you've already won, because so many people simply do not start. So you must start, you must continue, and you must not quit. Perseverance. An old Welsh proverb states that "without perseverance, talent is a barren bed."

Many people don't start because they think they may fail. But failure is certain if you don't start. So you must start. Herbert Kaufman said, "Failure is only postponed success as long as courage coaches ambition. The habit of persistence is the habit of victory."

Whatever necessity lays upon you to endure, whatever it commands, do. Start the task, continue the task. Don't quit, and commit to finishing.

You are upon greatness, and you know it, and sometimes that greatness scares you. That fear is healthy, and it is okay. But do not let that fear prevent you from execution. Execution is four steps, my friends: you start, you continue, you don't quit, and ultimately you commit to finishing the task.

Execute the process. Execute your vision. Above all things, execution is necessary for kingdom building. When it's done, like Marvin Sapp, you will sing, "I'm so glad I made it—I made it through!"

Notes

Have you ever had a vision and tried to execute it?

What have you learned from previous failed attempts of executing your vision (or past projects)?

Who in your life speaks negatively about your vision?

What is the most challenging part of execution for you?

What is preventing you from the execution of a project or vision?

LEADERSHIP

You have to lead in order to build. Leadership is a funny thing, and there are so many leadership experts in the world.

It seems like everyone has a philosophy on leadership. Most people understand that to do great things, you must consider and take care of the small things. Leadership is required even in the small things. I personally don't believe there's any small thing. I personally believe that any task executed and accomplished leads to bigger tasks, whether it's for you or for someone else that you touch, empower, or impact. Whatever the case may be, leadership is necessary. Leadership is necessary once you have a vision inside you. Leadership is necessary for execution. Leadership is necessary for kingdom building.

I remember speaking with a group of students, and what I was trying to impress upon them is that they are leaders; they are not tomorrow's leaders, but they're leaders right now. That's a hard thing to grasp when you're twelve years old and you're going through whatever personal challenges that a twelve-year-old might be going through, both superficially as well as the things that we can't see. Leadership is necessary. *All* of us are leaders and have inherent leadership gifts, talents, and abilities that can be either exposed or developed (or both) for us to become better leaders. Let me be clear—we are all leaders and have latent gifts waiting for us to step into our leadership roles. Let me say it another way: *you are a leader*. Have you ever quit? Failed? Perhaps you're quiet and shy. Maybe you don't like people. Maybe you've been abused or bullied. Maybe you think you are too young or too old, or you have been mocked. Maybe you are a recluse. Perhaps you have been very successful. Maybe you have a string of broken relationships. Maybe you have uncontrollable anger. We are *all* children of God born with a purpose that permeates through us—we are perfectly prepared to lead. It does not matter what challenge you have ever had in life. It does not matter what hill you are facing. Lead anyway!

You are a leader. Lead.

Many people ask the question, "How do I become this leader?" For me, when I speak to people and when I have conversations with people, I make sure that whomever I'm having a conversation with understands that he or she is next up.

This person is the next leader. This person's time to lead is right now.

If you ask me what *next up* means, it means that you ask great questions. Next up. I do want to make sure that all people who lead—which should be in the particular areas that they need to lead—understand that they're next up. I'm an acronym guy. I took NEXT UP, and I broke it down. The *N* in *NEXT UP* stands for *now*. Your time to lead is right now; it's not tomorrow. It's not next week. It's not next year. It's now. How do you know? And how you do that?

You must get MAD—Make A Decision. Make a decision to embrace the fact that you're next up and that your time to lead is now.

The *EX* in *NEXT UP* stands for *expert*. It takes about ten thousand hours to become an expert in any particular area. Now guess what? If you keep living, ten thousand hours will pass by. The question becomes this: what do we do with our time? Are we focused in any particular areas, or are we flippant? Are we doing so many things that we can't bear down in any particular areas? I'm a believer in using very accurate weapons—a bow and arrow. It's a single shot versus using a shotgun, spraying everything out wide, and fanning out our efforts. I believe you can be an expert in multiple areas, but I believe you need to conquer one area first. Expert. Take that time, and focus. Hone in on one particular area. What is your gift? What is the vision? What pulls on you? What is your passion? What is that thing that you would do for free?

I'm going to do this because I love to do it. I realized by the time I was fifteen that I loved to give advice. I would give advice to anyone who appeared to be struggling or came to me and said, "I am struggling. Kevin Suber, help me out of this. Kevin Suber, I don't know where to start. Kevin Suber, how'd you get that name?" I love to help people. I would help people with anything, no matter what. I would do that for free. It just so happens I no longer do that for free. I've become an expert in helping people to see things that they can't see themselves, small pockets around them. I became an expert in that—an expert counselor. What is that area for you?

The *T* is for *time*. When you look around, when you think about it, if I asked you to jot down the resources that you have, one of the most frequently missed resources is time. But here's what interesting about that resource of time: it is the only irreplaceable resource. I can make a billion dollars and lose it and make it back. I can have a house; if the house burns to the ground, I can build another house.

There's a story in the Bible about a man named Job who went through everything—trial after trial after trial. Job lost it all and got it all back. In fact, he got back more than he lost. Any resource that we lose, we can get back—except time. So what are you doing with your time? With whom are you spending your time? Time is the most valuable commodity because it is irreplaceable.

The *N* is for *now*. *EX* is for *expert*. *T* is for *time*. *U* is for *under*, and it has a dual meaning. I believe that you should always have somebody in front of you, an expert, somebody in an arena that knows more than you know but that's gone in the direction you happen to be going. You should be walking side by side with somebody who's going through challenges and struggles and victories with you, a peer or peers. I also believe you should always be reaching back, pulling somebody behind you and helping him or her to get through the things that you have already been through. That *U* in *NEXT UP* is *under*; you should always be under someone. You should always be getting information from someone who's done something that you haven't done, and you should always have somebody underneath you. You should always be mentoring and coaching and teaching and discipling. That's a simultaneous *U*. You're helping somebody to learn and go through the battles and struggles and victories that you've already had.

The last thing I'll leave you with is the most important thing of all. It ties into our last chapter about execution and getting started. The *P* in *NEXT UP* indicates that you are "perfectly prepared for your purpose." Everything you have gone through in your life up until right now has prepared you to lead now. To be an expert now. To take care of your time now. To be under now. To mentor somebody now. You are perfectly prepared for your purpose. Ladies and gentlemen, you all are next up. And your time to lead is now!

Notes

Are you a leader? Why or why not?

Whom do you consider to be a great leader?

If you could spend an afternoon with anyone, past or present, who would make you a better leader? Who is it, and why?

Are you an expert in any area?

Do you have a mentor? Do you have a mentee?

Name a challenge from your past that prevented you from starting a project or from growing your ability to lead.

OVERCOMING CHALLENGES

As long as you live, as long as there is air in your lungs, there are two things that are constant. The first thing is that you have purpose because you are still alive; therefore, your mission is not done. The second thing is if you are alive, you are in one of three places: you have just come out of a challenge, you are currently walking through a challenge, or you are headed into a challenge. You have just come out of the storm, you are currently in a storm, or you are headed into a storm.

That is life.

This is what happens; these are challenges that we must overcome. If I were to stop and reflect for a moment, I would think of the fact that when I was born, I had my umbilical cord around my neck, and my face was blue. Immediately, I was placed in an emergency situation just so that I could live. Just so that I could live. I had a defect in one of my legs, so I had to wear special shoes, and I remember my mom telling me as I was older that it broke her heart to see me in these shoes, but it was necessary for me to deal with that, to endure that (and for my mother to endure that) so that I could walk normally later. Fast-forward to high school, where I had a school record, believe it or not, in track and field. So not only did I learn to walk, but I also learned to run.

Growing up I had the normal challenges that people have: monetary challenges, the neighborhood bully, school challenges, the things that young men and young women face—especially getting into college or not getting into college, or deciding to go to college, or maybe picking the wrong college. All of these things we must face as we continue to live, and we are always in one of three states: coming out of a storm, in a storm, or headed into a storm. There's power, there's a lesson, in falling down.

Falling down is not failure. Not getting up *is* failure.

In all things that we do, we must learn to overcome challenges. Falling down is not failure; staying down is failure.

If you are alive, you will fall, accidentally or maybe by choice, maybe by things that you control and maybe by things you do not control. Falling down is not failure. Staying down is failure. Challenges are coming. The question becomes very simple: How do we overcome challenges?

There's a scene in a movie that I can see right now, and it's the very end scene of *The Pursuit of Happyness*, after Will Smith's character is offered a job. There's a sea of people all around, and the camera zeroes in on him, and you can see the joy on his face because of all the challenges he had to overcome.

And he's simply clapping. He's clapping.

As we go through life, we know the challenges are coming. You may say, "Okay, Kev; I know challenges are coming. How do I overcome challenges? I need a tool. I need a set of tools."

I have an acronym to refer to the tools that I give the people to overcome challenges: CLAP. You are to clap through challenges. Understand that life brings storms.

Before we get to CLAP and clapping, let's look at storms. The interesting thing about storms is when we observe storms that are far away, we see that they can be beautiful; they can be interesting. They can be all sorts of things. But when the storm is above us, when we're in the storm, it's very different. We become fearful. We become pressed or concerned because now it's a personal storm.

So whether it's observing a storm and giving somebody else the tools to overcome his or her storm or it is your own personal storm, how we get through that storm, how we get through those challenges, is this: we CLAP. We clap through storms because our personal storms, our personal struggles, our personal challenges are different. Those storms, those struggles, those obstacles must be overcome.

The *C* in *CLAP* stands for *change*. In order to get through a storm, in order to overcome a challenge, we must change. But it's not changing any portion of who we are. We must change in totality. We must change our entire beings. Change must permeate throughout our bodies, our mindsets, our relationships—through everything. We must change by connecting; we must connect with our souls to change.

Sometimes you have to impose your will on your soul and say, "Yes, that happened, but now I'm moving from here to there." You acknowledge it, and you move. We must connect with our souls to change. We must connect with our minds. Sometimes it is a simple as an affirmation: that happened; I'm now here. We must connect with our spirits.

Certain things will happen. Challenges will happen; they will bring you down. That's okay. That is natural. We must get through that. We must also impose our wills on our spirits the same way we impose our wills on our souls. Sometimes—and this is the biggest challenge—we have to change the people with whom we are connecting. Sometimes the people around us don't have the ability to move us forward, but they certainly have the ability to keep us stationary or stagnant, or they even have the ability to put us back into old, dangerous, bad, destructive habits that caused the challenges in the first place. The hard part is when we have to change the people.

Jim Rohn said, "Show me the people in a person's life, and show me what they're reading, and I can tell you where they'll be in five years." What are you reading, and who is in your life? If they don't project growth, then you can never overcome your challenges, and you will fall flat. The hard thing is to change the people.

That *C* also stands for *confess*. You must convincingly confess. Why? You must confess because you can't move past the point that caused the challenge until you acknowledge where you truly are. The first thing you have to do is confess what happened. You must confess convincingly to yourself. You may have to look in the mirror and say, "This is what happened." You must confess your current state.

"Okay, you know what? I had a lot of money; I spent it the wrong way. I am now broke."

"I had an opportunity to bid on a proposal, but I didn't do it quickly enough."

"I had an opportunity for a business opportunity, and I thought it would be there later. It was not."

You must convincingly confess what transpired in order to change. You must remind yourself of your purpose. What is your purpose? You must remind yourself of where you are going.

I used to run hurdles in high school. I never looked at the hurdle. I always looked at the finish line because the finish line was the goal; the hurdle was not the goal. If I looked at the hurdles, I hit the hurdles. You need to clear the hurdle and get to the finish line. That's the C.

L is for *look*.

So first we must change; then, we must look. We must look around and figure out where we are. Assess your situation; what is going on? Then take that a step further; ask, "What did I learn?"

"Okay, I just got $100,000. I quickly spent $98,000. I have $2,000 left. What did I learn? Maybe I shouldn't spend money that quickly. Maybe I should save some money. Right?"

"I ran hurdles; I tripped because I was so focused on the hurdle. Maybe I need to change what I focus on."

"This one person that's in my circle always brings me down. Whenever I'm around this person, I feel depressed. What did I learn? I learned that no matter how difficult it is, sometimes I must change the people in my circle. How can I prevent this from happening again?"

The L in *CLAP* is for *look*. After we have changed and committed to change, and we have looked around and assessed our situations, that's great, but that's all theory.

You must now take action, and the *A* in *CLAP* stands for *action*. Take action with accountability. Take action with authority. Sometimes people ask, "How can how can this be my burden?" or "How can this be my mission?" or "How do I know this is for me to do?"

Why me? Why not you?

When we talked about leadership, we talked about your being perfectly prepared for your purpose. So why not you? You are as equipped, you are as able, as anyone that you know. So why not you?

The *P* is for *pivot*. We know challenges are coming. Great! When the challenges come, we have two choices: we can stay down, we can stay stuck in that challenge, or we can pivot. You can say, "Yes, this happened; yes, okay, I looked and assessed where I am. What did I learn? Okay, now I'm going to take action." Well, taking action requires that you don't go in the same direction that caused the challenge in the first place. We pivot. We change direction; we course-correct. We move.

Sometimes, it's as simple as changing direction in your mind. You have to look in the mirror and say to yourself, "I was going that way; that is no longer possible. I am now going this way." Whatever it takes, you must shake it off. You pivot. You shake it off. Maybe it's writing a new plan. Maybe you had a plan that is impossible now or is possible. That *P* is for *plan*.

Maybe it's modifying your existing plan. What got you to where you are was only for the purpose of your learning what you needed to learn. Great! You learned it, and that pivot involves writing a new plan.

James Allen wrote a book called *As a Man Thinketh*. If you have not read this book, you should. It's about our thoughts and how powerful are thoughts are. He talks about prayer and meditation in this book. He talks about how a mind is a garden that can grow whatever seeds are planted there. So if prayer and meditation aren't part of what you do, then you need to add that to it; it's especially true when it comes time to change or to overcome challenges.

You have to meditate on those things that give you power, that give you life, that give you the ability to change, and course-correct, as opposed to thinking negative thoughts that will make you stand still or worse yet go backward. CLAP. We must pivot.

Overcoming challenges is hard. No one ever said it would be easy. Les Brown states, "If you do what is easy, your life will be hard. But if you do what is hard, your life will be easy."

I've given you some tools that hopefully will help you to overcome challenges. As long as you try, you are going to fall down. Just don't quit. As long as you try, there's a possibility of getting up. The only way you are sure not to get up is to not try. The most important thing I can tell you is as simple as the seven words that Jimmy Valvano said: "Don't give up. Don't ever give up."

CLAP. You clap through challenges.

Don't give up. Don't ever give up.

Notes

Name an incident or a challenge from your past that paralyzed you.

Write one thing you learned from that challenge.

Write one more thing you learned from that challenge.

Write a third thing that you learned from that challenge.

SUBER'S STORY

Everybody's struggle is different. As I continue to live, I understand that even with the challenges that I went through, as hard as they were for me, somebody else went through something even more challenging.

That is life.

There was a point in my life when I came home for Christmas. But before Christmas, my brother was killed in a car accident.

I carried a burden because I had the option of going home first, and I decided to go somewhere else first. That night my brother was out with friends; he was hit by a car that jumped a curve. That car struck the car my brother was in, and he died.

In the next four years after that, both my mother and my father died. So within five and a half years, I lost my mother, father, and brother.

I was newly married, and if I'm telling the truth, that put my brain, my soul, and my spirit into a flat spin. Every single project I was working on at that time stopped.

I didn't know what to do. There were times when I would drive, and I would have to pull the car over because I was overwhelmed with grief.

And I cried, and I cried, and I cried. I said, "Why did this happen? I don't understand this. Why did this happen?"

It affected everything in me. It affected my ability to move. It affected my ability to inspire other people. It affected my ability to be a good husband. It affected my ability to be a good father. It permeated the depths of my soul.

It crushed me.

And one day, I realized that it could no longer control me, because at the end of the day, there were people who were depending on me simply to do something like stand up. Give somebody a hug. Say good morning. Earn an income. I was happy to be able to earn fifteen dollars an hour.

I now consult for significantly more than that.

Why am I sharing this? Because as challenging as that story may sound for some of you, others have been through so much worse. Life will throw the curveballs, the sliders, and all sorts of pitches that you cannot hit. They might even smack you in the head and knock you down.

That's life.

Get up.

THE FOUR PILLARS: YOUR FOUNDATION

I had something interesting happen to me a few years ago.

I got a phone call from a friend—a fraternity brother and also a business partner—telling me that he had submitted me to be a panelist and to speak at a leadership event. The majority of his reason for doing so was that I was one of the few people he knew who actually had done business internationally, and he thought that my perspective, specifically for leaders and entrepreneurs, would be a great one.

I remember when he said that, I thought, "Wow, okay. Well, this sounds exciting! I'm going to go if they ask me to." They did ask me to go, and I went, and I had a great time. And I took the advice of many people around me with respect to preparation before I got there, making sure my social media stuff was up to date, making sure my latest information was correct on my business cards, and so forth—things that I normally would tell other people at this point.

When I went, I had a phenomenal time and ended up staying for the entire conference. It was the NAACP L500 conference, a leadership conference. It was amazing. While I was there, there was a young lady who was listening to my commentary about being an entrepreneur and about coaching. She found me on Twitter and approached me afterward, and we had a conversation. She said, "I want to talk to you about what you do because I believe I need you."

I laughed because that's what my wife and my children say to me: "We need you." That conversation opened a door to another business of mine that still goes on today and is an integral part of it: my business of coaching. I ended up coaching her, we had a great time and great success, and she's doing phenomenal things. She also opened the door to several other people to do something that I'd already been doing, but in a more structured way.

Through that process, I developed the cornerstone of my coaching process: the four pillars. Whenever I coach anybody, I make sure that I coach with respect to this. When I'm coaching you, whether in business or any particular area of your life, it boils down to the four pillars.

The reason why I call it "the four pillars" is that when all four of these are operating the way they should be operating, then life is grand, even in the midst of challenges. But if any of them are off, that's like a triangle missing one leg; it starts to crumble, and it crumbles quickly. (And by the way, it does not look good or feel good. It's really, really bad.)

Here are the four pillars, in no particular order, and they must function well: your interpersonal skills, your spirit life, your business or vocational life, and your health and wellness.

If any one of these is off, it affects the other pillars, and then there is a crash. The crash can sometimes be quick and can be painful.

I'm going to start with interpersonal skills, because at the end of the day, we are social beings.

You're born. The first thing you do is you look in your mother's eyes, and you're cooing, and she's looking at you, and everything is grand—until you get to kindergarten or the playground and you meet that jerk, and that starts to affect how you interact with people from that point forward.

One of the more important things that we can learn in life is how we handle and manage our interpersonal skills. At the end of this book, there's going to be a glossary of books that I believe in (in no particular order) that will help you do some great things with respect to self-reflection and study in the areas of the four pillars. You'll see some books at the end that will help you with interpersonal skills.

But know this: if you don't know how to have a normal conversation with a person, if you don't know how to interact with people and feel comfortable—the Dale Carnegie book title is *How to Win Friends and Influence People*, right?—if you don't know how to do that, to win friends and influence people in a positive and constructive way, then the interpersonal-skills portion of your life becomes very challenging. And when that happens, it will topple the other three pillars.

Let's look at your spiritual life, another pillar. It's no secret to anyone that a person who is successful understands that things that get done at a very high level do not happen solely because of him or her; it was more an example of getting things perfectly in place and then letting the spirit do what he or she could not.

I love the way John Maxwell says it: when you've done all that you can do, when you put everything in line, and you've organized the best that you can, and you built the best team—after you do all of that, then allow room for the supernatural. Not to become super religious, but we do realize that there are some things that happen, and we scratch our heads and say, "How did that happen?" Some people say the universe made it happen. Some people will say it was Allah, or God, or Jesus or Jeshua, or Buddha, etc. To be clear, for me, this is where I acknowledge Christ as the author and finisher of my faith, the one who filled in the blanks and gave direction when there was none. You can and should take time to fill in the blanks for yourself.

All the different supreme beings or spiritual beings have an impact. At the end of the day, the truth is as simple as this: there are some things that are going to happen external from our bodies, and we either pay attention to this and feel those forces and acquiesce and move to them and trust them, or we don't.

One of the simplest ways to become in tune with the spiritual component of yourself is as simple as praying and meditating. If you are not taking care of and naturally feeding the spiritual component of your existence, it will affect the other three pillars. Your spiritual life is one of the four pillars.

Your business or vocation is one of the four pillars. The business component is such a critical piece that for many, we identify and we define our success or our failures by how we are doing with our businesses and with our vocations.

I saw a very interesting video on social media that was from a young lady, and she recapped the conversation she had had with Sallie Mae. She basically said, "I got my degree. I cannot become employed. I'm not feeling very good about myself; therefore, I think this degree was a waste of my time. Since I cannot turn my degree in, because I already got it and they won't accept it back, I don't feel like I should have to pay you this money right now until I can become gainfully employed."

Now, of course, she was saying it out of jest, but the reality is that I have coached many like her; if they can't get the types of jobs that they want after graduation, it is highly frustrating for them. I would say that your business, your vocation, is one of the four pillars. It is something that must work very, very well for you, and if not, that not only becomes a point of contention and frustration, but it will also crumble the other three pillars.

Last, but certainly not least, is the pillar of health and wellness. You cannot walk in your calling if you cannot walk. It's really that simple. Your health must be taken care of.

I'm a graduate of the University of Virginia. There was a class about mental health that showed the connection between physical fitness and overall health and wellness and how well we learned and what the educational components of our lives looked like. They are intrinsically linked.

Many other studies looked at point guards, quarterbacks, and athletes who have to make very quick decisions, and there is a link between physical fitness and how the brain functions. Health and wellness are intrinsically intertwined, as is the success of every single person who is trying to function at an elite level. So you must do some very simple things. Please understand that health and wellness is not just exercise. One of the most critical components of health and wellness is what you're eating.

I don't want to preach to you, but do understand that you are not only what you eat; more accurately, you are what you absorb. Let me repeat that: you are what you absorb. Therefore, it's very important to know what you're eating and to know how food is absorbed into your body in conjunction with exercise. Health and wellness, diet and nutrition—those things go hand in hand.

It's like strength and conditioning—you not only need to push some weights around and do some sorts of push-ups and things of that nature, but you also need to make sure you sweat and get the heart pumping.

Stay focused on the four pillars, and continue to grow in those areas—your interpersonal relationships, your spiritual life, your business and vocational life, and of course health and wellness. When all four of those are functioning at such levels that you are continuing to push and press in those areas of your life, you see an exponential growth in your life in general.

People around you are happier, you are happier, you are thriving, you are growing, you are thrusting, and you are doing incredible things.

The most important thing that I want you to get at this juncture of this book is to understand that if you stay focused on the four pillars of your life, your life will grow exponentially.

I'm not one who is big on formulas—go figure, with my degree in engineering—but this is a formula that I know works well. One plus one plus one plus one—those four pillars equal a phenomenal life.

LEGACY

Everyone should passionately desire to leave a legacy.

We've walked through several chapters in this book, ultimately to inspire you to do two things: (1) build your kingdom, and (2) leave your legacy.

Your kingdom should be built with the mind-set of leaving a legacy that transforms lives. After you read the last page of this book, my hope is that you will put it down, close your eyes, and envision a kingdom that would be transformative for everyone who lived there.

I had a conversation with a friend, and he talked about the power of images and imagination. He talked about how whatever you imagine is real, and when you think about how great things are invented, you know that to be true.

Someone first has to imagine it. Someone first has to dream it.

Then, there are the questions of how we can execute the dreams, how we can execute the visions, how we continue to go when we have obstacles. How do we overcome those obstacles and challenges? Whom do we lead in this mission with us? How do we inspire others?

All of this is done ultimately not just to build something special, and that's part of it, but that special thing that is built should leave a legacy.

This morning I cried because I desire to transform as many lives as possible. I cry because my desire is so strong that I would hope that anyone and everyone who could ever hear my voice or could ever see words that I have written would be inspired to do something not just for themselves but for the purpose of transforming others. Legacy. What is the call on your life that leaves something behind? What is it that you will do that will transform, inspire, and change others?

When you build your kingdom, don't build your kingdom for you. Build your kingdom with the whole promise and purpose of leaving a legacy. Put your crown on. Build your kingdom. Leave your legacy!

Thank you for reading these words.

Notes

What do you want to leave behind for the benefit of others?

Which of your gifts and talents will be needed to accomplish this?

Who has different gifts and talents that are different from yours that can help you accomplish this?

Who will benefit from this legacy you leave?

GLOSSARY OF SUGGESTED READING

The Bible

The 7 Habits of Highly Effective People, by Stephen Covey

The 10 Best Decisions a Leader Can Make, by Bill Farrel

The 21 Irrefutable Laws of Leadership, by John C. Maxwell

As a Man Thinketh, by James Allen

The Compound Effect, by Darren Hardy

Navigating the Heart: Who Is Dragging You?, by Ock Soo Park

The Power of Money, by Kenneth Ulmer

The Slight Edge, by Jeff Olson

Today Matters, by John C. Maxwell

ACKNOWLEDGMENTS

There was a boulder—a large boulder—that had to be pushed up a hill. I was the only one assigned to push this boulder up the hill. It was an impossible assignment on my own, but thank God I had help. That boulder is in your hands right now.

I thank God for trusting me to move this boulder and then giving me the words to start the boulder moving.

I thank my wife, Nicole, for her support—the support needed to continue pushing the boulder.

I thank my children, Naomi, Isaiah, Hannah, and Hezekiah, for their patience while I continued to push this boulder.

I thank my parents, John and Goldie Suber, for pushing boulders so I would know that pushing a boulder was possible.

I thank John Taylor for helping me develop the skill set to move this boulder.

I thank Luis Lopez for helping to capture the words that were disguised as a boulder.

KEVIN J. SUBER

I thank God again for giving me insight to realize this boulder was actually made of many seeds that were gathered during my journey.

I thank all of you for eating the fruit of this boulder.

God bless you, enjoy, and bon appétit.

#leadanyway #coachKev #kingdombusiness #licensedtolead

AUTHOR BIO

KEVIN J. SUBER
SEVANT, ENTREPRENEUR, SPEAKER, COACH

Born in New Haven, CT, Kevin attended Hopkins High School and then graduated with a degree in Civil Engineering from the University of Virginia. After Graduation, Kevin worked for a small shipyard in Norfolk Virginia called the Jonathan Corporation. Moving through various departments as part of the engineering training program, Mr. Suber ultimately had oversight of 7 department heads and 175 people – at the age of 26. After completing his assignment, Kevin moved on to work for Texaco. While at Texaco, Kevin served in various capacities as part of an executive training/fast track program. Mr. Suber served in three of the 6 US lubricants plants Texaco had at that time. While at corporate headquarters, Kevin had oversight of a $15MM budget for Capital Expenditure and Environmental Remediation.

After 15 years in corporate America, the entrepreneurial spirit lead to the formation of The Suber Group – an entertainment company. Over time, the focus of the company expanded from talent management and Electronic Press Kit production to include film production, market research, marketing and promotions. Always a passionate entrepreneur, Mr. Suber started several businesses in the health and wellness arena which lead to some international business experience.

Outside of business, Kevin is a member of Faithful Central Bible Church (FCBC) in Inglewood, CA. Faithful Central has a membership of approximately 8,000. While at FCBC Kevin served in the (offering) counting ministry. This led to being asked to serve in the Deacon Ministry. Kevin had oversight of Men's Discipleship and served as the church's assistant Treasurer. Kevin's duties as a Deacon and as the assistant treasurer would frequently lead to interface with the logistics team and the Usher ministry as well. Kevin's position as assistant treasurer also resulted in frequent interaction with the churches CFO as well as the churches Elder Board. The Elders at FCBC in conjunction with the CFO make all the financial decisions for that Church. Mr. Suber also helped to launch a new church (A Place for Worship in Fullerton, CA) and served as the chairman of the board of directors for three years.

The breadth of knowledge gained in multiple disciplines led to being recognized as an expert in leadership, entrepreneurship and mindset. Kevin is now a sought-after speaker and a Life/Executive Coach that works with executives, groups and individuals in the area of personal, professional and spiritual growth as well as leadership training and coaching. Kevin has been invited to speak for organizations such as Shaw University, The NAACP, Meals on Wheels and IYF (International Youth Fellowship) to name a few.

Kevin is married with 4 children and resides in Los Angeles, CA

Made in the USA
Middletown, DE
10 February 2025